Style Secrets

NAIL CARE

TIPS & TRICKS

EMMA CARLSON BERNE

ILLUSTRATED BY ELENA HESCHKE

Lerner Publications ◆ Minneapolis

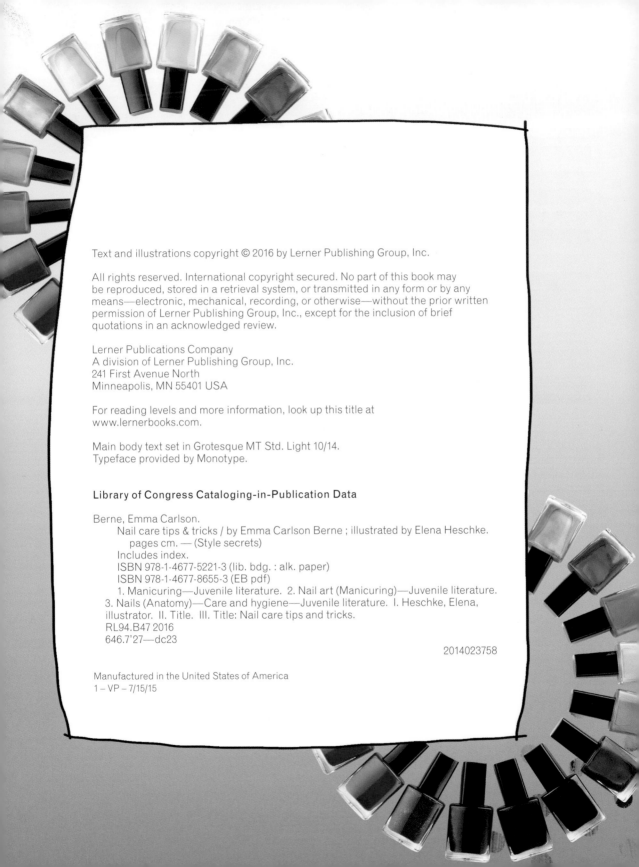

Lerner Publications Company
A division of Lerner Publishing Group, Inc.
241 First Avenue North
Minneapolis, MN 55401 USA

For reading levels and more information, look up this title at www.lernerbooks.com.

Main body text set in Grotesque MT Std. Light 10/14.
Typeface provided by Monotype.

Library of Congress Cataloging-in-Publication Data

Berne, Emma Carlson.
    Nail care tips & tricks / by Emma Carlson Berne ; illustrated by Elena Heschke.
        pages cm. — (Style secrets)
    Includes index.
    ISBN 978-1-4677-5221-3 (lib. bdg. : alk. paper)
    ISBN 978-1-4677-8655-3 (EB pdf)
    1. Manicuring—Juvenile literature. 2. Nail art (Manicuring)—Juvenile literature.
3. Nails (Anatomy)—Care and hygiene—Juvenile literature. I. Heschke, Elena,
illustrator. II. Title. III. Title: Nail care tips and tricks.
    RL94.B47 2016
    646.7'27—dc23

                                                                2014023758

Manufactured in the United States of America
1 – VP – 7/15/15

Introduction

TOUGH AS NAILS?

Imagine trying to scratch your nose without a fingernail. How about dropping a book on your toe without the protection of a toenail? Fingernails and toenails are crucial tools. They also protect the ends of our digits. But they aren't just useful. With manicures and pedicures, fingernails and toenails can be painted wild colors, stamped with designs, decorated with stickers, or even studded with tiny jewels. Painting and decorating your nails is like making a tiny art project right on your hands or feet.

What are the secrets to glamorous nails? You're about to find out. If you take good care of your nails' health as well as their looks, you'll be a nail expert in no time. And you'll be ready to turn your nails into expressions of your personal style.

Chapter 1

NEAT NAILS AND HEALTHY HANDS

All fingernails and toenails have a few important parts. The nail plate is the hard, nonliving top layer. The nail bed is the soft skin underneath. The nail tip is the part of the plate that extends beyond the nail bed. This is the part you clip when it gets too long. The cuticle is the gummy tissue that connects your skin to your nail at the bottom and on the sides. Each separate part contributes to a nail's overall health. And nails look best when they're healthy.

It's easy to spot an unhealthy nail. It might be bumpy, ridged, discolored, or unusually thick. The cuticles might be cracked or flaky. And if dirt or germs get in the wrong places, a nail can get infected, which is painful as well as unsightly. But here's the good news: It's not hard to treat your nails right. And if you do, they'll look as good as they feel.

Not Too Long, Not Too Short . . . Just Right!

Make sure you don't let your nails grow too long. Very long nails can interfere with basic activities, like typing or eating. Long nails also break easily and can collect grime.

But you also want to avoid cutting your nails too short. This can lead to painful ingrown nails. File each nail until it extends just past the tip of your finger. That's long enough to be safe and stylish without getting in the way.

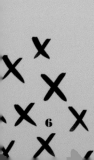

6

KEEPING CLEAN

Just like washing your face or combing your hair, taking care of your fingernails and toenails is an important part of hygiene. Nails need to be cleaned, trimmed, and filed. Keeping the skin on your hands and feet clean and smooth also helps keep you healthy.

Trim your fingernails about once a week and your toenails about every two weeks. Every time you wash your hands, rub a little soap under your fingernails too. Keep a nailbrush in the shower and give your toenails a good scrub when you wash your feet.

Help! I Bite My Nails

Nail-biting is a very common problem. Many people bite their nails from stress, nervousness, or just habit. But biting your nails for a long time can damage your nail bed. This can make nails permanently bumpy or discolored. Your hands are also more likely to get infections from tiny wounds around the nails.

If you want to stop biting your nails, first cut them very short, so there will not be much to bite. Then try dabbing chili oil or lemon juice on your nails. The unpleasant taste can help you train yourself to stop biting. Often just painting your nails with clear nail polish helps. Nail polish tastes pretty bad! If you're still having no luck, talk to a doctor, a school nurse, or a school counselor about other ways to stop biting your nails. You may need to deal with the bigger issues, such as stress, that are causing the problem.

NAIL TOOLS

Fingernails that are dirty, broken, or bumpy don't present you at your best and aren't good for your overall health. The same goes for dirty or rough skin around your nails. So how do you keep your nails, hands, and feet in top shape? It's simple. You'll just need a few basic supplies to get you started.

<u>Clippers and scissors.</u> You can trim your fingernails with nail scissors or with nail clippers. Nail scissors are small and have curved blades. The blades will help you follow the curved shape of your fingernail as you trim. Toenails should always be cut with nail clippers—or nail "nippers," which have straight jaws instead of the curved jaws of regular clippers. With nippers, you can more easily avoid trimming nails too short. With clippers or nippers, make several small cuts in a straight line across the nail. Don't use one long cut to trim a nail. This can damage the nail plate.

<u>Nail files.</u> A nail file can replace clippers for fingernail trimming if you use it often. You can get a metal file or disposable emery boards. An emery board is a cardboard strip with sandpaper-like material on both sides. One side is rough for quick filing, and the other side is finer for smoothing out rough spots. When you file your fingernails, use long strokes going in one direction. Don't use a sawing, back-and-forth stroke. That can weaken the nail, causing it to split or break.

<u>Nailbrush.</u> A nailbrush is good for scrubbing stubborn dirt and oil out from under your nails. Rinse it thoroughly after every use and hang it to dry. Every few weeks, run it through the dishwasher to clean it.

<u>Pumice stone.</u> This small chunk of lightweight, porous rock can rub off the rough skin on your hands and feet, revealing the softer new skin underneath. Get it damp before you use it. When you're finished, rinse it thoroughly under warm water. Then use an old toothbrush and some dish detergent to scrub the stone clean. Store it in a dry, airy place.

<u>Soothers.</u> A bottle of basic hand lotion will keep the skin on your fingers and toes smooth. Baby oil moisturizes your cuticles. Stock up on cotton balls and Q-tips to apply and remove these and other products.

BASIC NAIL TRIM AND GROOMING

Are your nails due for a trim? Make it really count with a little extra care.

What You Need:

- soap
- a nailbrush
- nail clippers or nail scissors
- a nail file or an emery board
- a Q-tip
- baby oil
- hand lotion

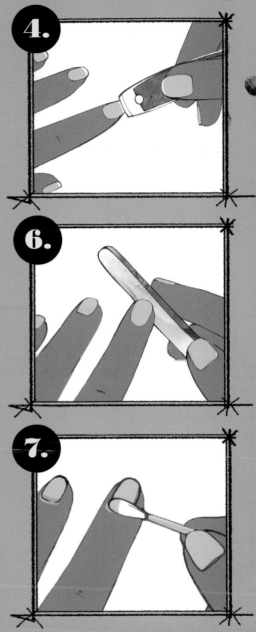

Here's How:

1. Wash your hands and feet with soap in running water.

2. Scrub under your nails with the nailbrush.

3. Dry your feet and hands.

4. Clip your fingernails—first, the top and then the sides. Stay away from the edge of the nail bed. Try trimming your fingernails in an oval or a round-cornered square shape.

5. Clip your toenails straight across the top. Toenails should never be cut from the sides and should always be cut straight. This will prevent ingrown toenails.

6. Using the nail file or the emery board, rub short strokes in one direction across the top and the sides of each fingernail, smoothing out the rough or sharp corners.

7. Dip a Q-tip in baby oil and rub oil all over your cuticles to soften them. Let the oil soak in for a few moments.

8. Rub lotion into hands and feet.

HAPPY HANDS AND FEET

The most flawless nails in the world won't look or feel great if the skin around them isn't in good shape too. When the skin on your hands and feet gets too dry, it can develop cracks. These cracks can be painful and not very pleasant to look at. They can also let bacteria into your body. You can keep the skin on your hands and feet smooth and moisturized by using lotion after you get out of the shower or the bath every day.

If the skin on your hands and feet is very dry, slather on a thick layer of hand lotion at night, just before bed. Then cover your hands and your feet with socks. (That's right—put socks on your lotion-covered hands.) Sleep like this all night, and in the morning, take the socks off. Your hands and feet should feel as soft as lambs' ears.

Oils Are Essential

Essential oils are plant and flower oils, taken straight from the plant or the flower, with nothing added. Lavender, rose, peppermint, orange, and lemon are common essential oils. These oils have a strong scent, so you only need to add two or three drops to a mixture. And that's good, because essential oils can be expensive! They are usually sold in a glass bottle with a dropper. You can often find essential oils at bath and body stores or online.

EASY FOOT TREATMENT

A foot scrub is a great way to remove dead, dry skin and moisturize the fresh skin underneath. Do this activity in your bathroom with your feet in the bathtub if possible.

What You Need:

- a large basin or a plastic tub
- water
- 1 or 2 towels
- a small bowl
- a measuring cup and measuring spoons
- $\frac{1}{4}$ cup salt
- 2 tablespoons olive oil
- a spoon
- a washcloth or a washing mitten
- lotion

Here's How:

1. Fill the basin or the plastic tub with water and set it in your bathtub—or on the floor with a towel underneath.

2. Mix the salt and olive oil in the bowl. The mixture should look like very wet sand.

3. Sit on the edge of the bathtub or on a chair in front of the basin. Wet your feet in the basin.

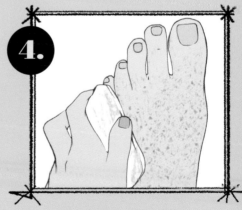

4. Using the washcloth or the washing mitten, rub the salt-oil mixture all over your damp feet. Scrub especially hard on the bottoms and sides of your feet, as well as your toes.

5. Rinse your feet well in running water and pat them dry.

6. Rub in some lotion. Your feet are perfectly moisturized and smooth!

Chapter 2

PICK YOUR POLISH

Ready for some serious nail style? You can use your basic nail care tools to make your feet and hands fabulous and fun. And if you want to paint your nails, head to the makeup aisle at your favorite retail store. Grab a bottle of polish remover and a few bottles of polish that you're keen to try.

CHOOSING NAIL POLISH

You know that nail polish comes in many different colors and shades. But are you familiar with all the different *types* of polish? You can find any look from sparkly to metallic. Here are a few common kinds to consider:

<u>Crème.</u> A crème is a basic, shiny nail polish. You can find it in all sorts of colors for every occasion. When you're going out with friends or to a party, let loose with bright neon colors or stunning black or white polish. For a subtler everyday look, try soft pink or beige—or clear polish, which just makes your nails shiny.

<u>Matte.</u> A matte nail polish is like a crème polish but without shine. It gives your nails a flat coat of color, similar to the sheen on a chalkboard. Mattes are a fun, bold look, but they can be harder to paint on than crème polishes, and they can chip more easily.

Matte

Jelly. Thicker than crèmes, jelly polishes are glossy and translucent. The first coat will be almost see-through, and you can apply as many as four more layers to build up the color.

Chrome. Many polishes give off a metallic sheen. Duochrome or multichrome polish contains several colors. The colors flash differently, depending on the reflection of the light. Iridescent polish is a softer version of duochrome.

Glitter. This high-impact polish usually consists of a clear base mixed with sparkles. The sparkly pieces can come in a variety of tiny shapes, from rectangles to stars. Holographic polish contains glitter that changes color under different lights.

Glass fleck. This type of polish looks as if it has tiny glass particles mixed with the base, creating an iridescent but smooth finish.

Shimmer. Very small flecks of glitter mixed into a basic nail polish create a subtle sparkle. Unlike with glitter polish, individual bits of sparkle can't be seen. You'll see just a smooth sheen. Frost polish is an extra-smooth form of shimmer.

Sheer. To add a transparent shine to your nails, try a sheer polish. These usually dry clear—or with just a hint of pink to match your nail's natural color.

If you're just starting out on your nail polish adventure, go with a few basic crèmes or mattes in shades you love. As you gain experience, you can expand your collection gradually.

Chrome

Glitter

Shimmer

STORING YOUR SUPPLIES

Your bottles of nail polish can last for two or three years after you open them, provided you follow a few key tips. Store your nail polish in a cool, dry, dark place, such as a closet or a closed box. Sunlight and moisture can discolor the polish. But don't put polish in the refrigerator! This can cause the polish to thicken and make it hard to apply. Always store bottles upright. If you put them on their sides, the pigments can separate, and it's harder to blend them back together.

In older polish, pigment can start to separate even if you're treating your bottles well. Polish also gets thicker with age. To remix aging polish, roll the bottle back and forth between your palms. You can also buy some nail polish thinner and add a few drops to stubborn older polish.

Bubble Trouble

Sometimes tiny bubbles appear in your polish and make even an expert manicure look bumpy. To prevent bubbles, avoid shaking your nail polish bottle before you use it. Instead, roll it back and forth between the palms of your hands. This will mix the color evenly, without creating pesky air pockets that show up as bubbles later.

NAIL POLISH COLOR CODING

If you have a lot of nail polish bottles stored in one box, it can take a while to find the shade or the type you're looking for. You have to lift up each bottle to read the label or check the shade. Or not! Color-code the tops of your bottles' lids so you can tell what's inside at a glance.

What You Need:

- your nail polish bottles
- small white address labels or plain white paper
- a hole punch or a pair of scissors
- craft glue, if using plain white paper
- a shoe box with a lid, any size

Here's How:

1. Swipe a small patch of each nail polish color on the address labels or on the plain paper. Leave space between each patch.

2. Allow polish patches to dry completely.

3. With the hole punch, punch out a circle of nail polish color from each patch. If you don't have a hole punch, you can cut out a circle with scissors.

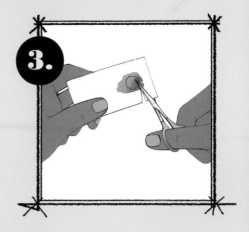

4. If you are using white labels, peel off the back and stick each circle to the top of the bottles' lids. If you are using plain paper, use a dot of craft glue to attach each circle.

5. Neatly line the bottles up in the shoe box. The next time you want some blue shimmer, just look for the shimmery blue dot!

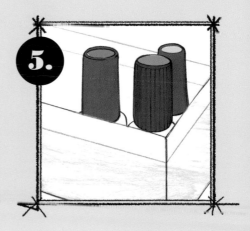

APPLICATION 101

Before you start painting your nails, find a place with good air circulation. Open a window if you're inside. Lay down a few paper towels or rags to catch any drips. You don't want your polish to stain your clothes, the carpet, or the countertop.

When you open a bottle of nail polish, scrape the brush on the side of the jar to prevent drips. Put the lid back on while you wait for applied polish to dry between coats. The less the polish is exposed to open air, the longer it'll last.

Use short up-and-down strokes to paint your nails. Start by applying a thin base coat. Let that dry. Then add one or two more thin coats. Wait for each layer to dry completely before you start the next coat. Don't make the layers too thick, or they'll take longer to dry and will clump more easily.

When you're finished painting, wipe the edge of the bottle clean and screw the cap on tightly. If any polish got on your cuticles or on the rest of your fingers, dip a Q-tip in nail polish remover and dab away the stray color.

Careful with Your Cuticles!

Cuticles may get in the way when you're painting your nails. But you should *never* trim your cuticles. This can lead to infection. Instead, you can gently, carefully push back your cuticles with the round edge of an emery board or with a cuticle pusher, which you can find in stores. Do this right after a shower or after you've moisturized the cuticles with baby oil.

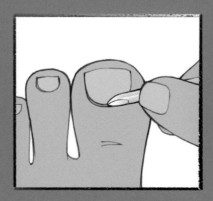

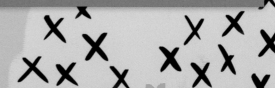

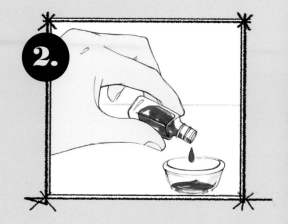

GLITTER NAIL POLISH

Glitter nail polish is a fun way to dress up your nails. You can buy it in a store, of course, but why not make your own? It's much more fun. And it's easy to do. You can use the same kind of basic glitter that works for craft projects. Pair it with a light shade of nail polish if you want the glitter to show up clearly. Or if you pick a dark nail polish color, use a light shade of glitter. For instance, try silver glitter on deep red polish.

What You Need:

- a teaspoon
- basic glitter
- a small bowl
- crème or matte nail polish
- a toothpick or a Q-tip

Here's How:

1. Measure about a teaspoon of glitter into a bowl that you no longer use for food.

2. Pour in about the same amount of nail polish (without using the measuring spoon). It's fine to have a little more or less glitter and a little more or less polish.

3. Stir the mixture with the toothpick or a Q-tip.

4. Working quickly, before the polish dries, paint your nails their new glittery shade.

Chapter 3

MANIS AND PEDIS

Manicures and pedicures are some of the easiest ways to get creative with your nails while also giving them the care they need. And you can give yourself these treatments at home instead of spending money at a salon. Setting aside an hour or so for nail-pampering every few weeks will help keep your nails healthy and give you a chance to experiment with polish.

Gather your nail tools and nail polish. Then find a clean, relaxing place to work. Your bathroom is perfect. (But if you share a bathroom with others in your family, let them know you'll be in there for about thirty minutes, and ask if anyone needs to get in first.) You can also take a large basin of water into your bedroom. Just spread out a large towel to catch spills.

Always start a manicure and a pedicure with clean nails. Soak your hands or feet in a basin full of water for five to ten minutes. (While you're at it, you can add a few drops of essential oil to the water for a fragrant bonus.) Use a nailbrush to clean under your nails if you need to. Does the skin on your feet feel rough or dry? You might have a buildup of dead skin. Consider using a pumice stone. Make sure your feet are wet and soapy, and then wet the stone. Rub the stone firmly all over the bottoms and sides of your feet, then rinse, and pat your feet dry.

Next, it's time for the real deal. Get ready to relax. This isn't a time to rush. A manicure or a pedicure is basically a two-part activity. Part 1 is grooming your nails. Part 2 is painting them. During part 2, you'll have to wait for your polish to dry, so put on some of your favorite music. Or if you're doing a pedi, have a book or a magazine handy. (You should try not to move your nails while their polish is drying, so for manis, plan for hands-free entertainment.) Take your time, and enjoy the process as much as the result.

Just Add Moisture!

Have you ever had a hangnail? Those pesky torn bits of skin that show up next to fingernails and toenails seem to be begging you to pull them out. But don't do it! Pulling out a hangnail risks tearing the skin more and even causing infection. To remove a hangnail, cut it at the base with a pair of clean clippers or nail scissors. You can help prevent them by applying moisturizing lotion to your nails and cuticles along with the rest of your hands and feet.

FRENCH MANICURE

A French manicure brings out your natural nail colors. The tip of the nail (the white part) is painted with white nail polish that follows the natural upside-down smile shape of the nail tip. The rest of the nail is usually painted beige or just left natural.

What You Need:

- nail clippers
- an emery board or a nail file
- a Q-tip (optional)
- baby oil (optional)
- rubbing alcohol
- a cotton ball
- white nail polish
- nail polish remover

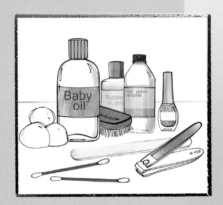

Here's How:

1. Clip each nail in the shape of a soft, rounded oval.

2. With the emery board or the nail file, smooth the rough edges of the nail, using short strokes in one direction.

3. If you like, dip a Q-tip in baby oil, and rub it all over your cuticles. Let the oil soak in a moment.

4. Put a bit of rubbing alcohol on the cotton ball, and wipe your nails to remove any trace of baby oil.

CONTENTS

Introduction
Tough as Nails? 4

Chapter 1
Neat Nails and Healthy Hands 6

Chapter 2
Pick Your Polish 12

Chapter 3
Manis and Pedis 18

Chapter 4
Nail Art 24

The Real Secret 29

Glossary 30

Further Information 31

Index 32

TREATING YOUR TOENAILS

You may not show off your feet as often as your fingertips. But in warm weather, open-toed shoes give you a chance to display those nails. That's extra incentive to keep your toenails in prime condition!

BASIC PEDICURE WITH POLISH

Treat your toes to a refreshing round of cleaning, soothing, and nail painting. You'll feel as if you're at the spa!

What You Need:

- nail clippers
- an emery board
- baby oil (optional)
- cotton balls
- Q-tips
- rubbing alcohol
- nail polish

Here's How:

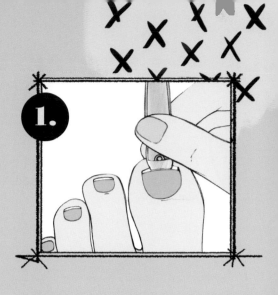

1. Clip your toenails straight across the top and just above the nail bed. Do not clip the sides of the nails.

2. File the nails with the emery board until they are smooth and straight.

3. If you'd like, paint your cuticles with baby oil. Then use the cotton ball and rubbing alcohol to wipe off any traces of oil.

4. Paint your toenails.

5. If the polish drips onto your skin, dab the drips with a dry Q-tip. If the drips have already dried, dip a Q-tip in a little rubbing alcohol to remove nail polish from your skin.

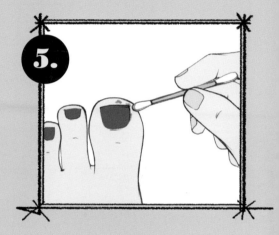

6. Don't wear shoes or socks for fifteen minutes.

7. Gently touch the nails to see if they are dry.

8. If you'd like, repeat steps 4 through 7 to apply a second coat.

Room to Breathe

Toenails don't like being crammed into shoes that are too small for them. They need room to grow. If they're constantly rubbing against the insides of shoes, you may start to see damage, such as swelling of the toe, bruising under the nail, or thickening of the nail. Make sure your shoes are the right size for your feet, and keep your nails trimmed so that they don't overcrowd your shoes.

Chapter 4
NAIL ART

Are you comfortable grooming and painting your nails? Then you're ready for the next level of decoration—nail art. You can create designs on each nail, using the nailbrush as a paintbrush and the nail polish as paint.

Creating unique nail art can be easy as well as fun. Use Q-tips to make soft, feathery dots and toothpicks to make tiny, more solid dots. Cut masking tape into tiny strips, and use it to make clean stripes across your nails after you paint over it. Do you have circular hole reinforcements for binder pages? Lay those on your nails and paint over them. Then remove them. You'll see half-moons or curvy stripes. If you have an old liquid eyeliner brush, clean it thoroughly, and use it as a very precise paintbrush. Or use an old, clean eye shadow brush to make a swirly design. Lay a paper towel on top of your nail, paint over it, and let the nail polish soak through to make a snakeskin pattern.

Take some risks. Try out different ideas. Mess up. You can always remove a mistake—or you may find that mistakes lead to your greatest creative successes.

FLOWERS ON YOUR FINGERNAILS

Want to paint a fun design on your nails but not sure where to start? A flower pattern adds color and pizzazz. With this activity, you can paint all your nails at once for a uniform design, or you can vary the look on each nail.

What You Need:

- nail clippers
- a nail file
- a light shade of non-glittery nail polish
- 3 darker shades of non-glittery nail polish
- wax paper
- Q-tips
- toothpicks

Here's How:

1. Prepare your nails by cutting and filing them.

2. Paint your nails all over with your light shade of polish.

3. Wait for the polish to dry, about ten minutes.

4. Pour out a small puddle of each darker shade of polish on a piece of wax paper. Do not let the three puddles touch one another.

5. Working quickly, dip one end of the Q-tip in one puddle of polish and dab the Q-tip in the middle of your nail. The polish should form a dot, which will be the center of the flower. Repeat with the other nails of that hand if you want the same design for all of them.

6. Dip the end of a toothpick in another color of polish. Carefully dab four smaller dots around the middle dot to make the petals. Think of the middle dot as a clock, and dab the four dots at twelve, three, six, and nine o'clock. (Repeat on other nails if you wish.)

7. Dip a fresh toothpick in the last puddle of polish, and make four more dots in the spaces between the first dots. These are the last of the flower petals. (Repeat on other nails if you wish.)

8. Let the paint dry and repeat on the rest of your fingers. You can mix up the color combinations for some variety. Then enjoy your flowery hands!

STICK-ON STYLE

Nail decals and stickers are another fun way to create nail art. Glue on nail ornaments for some added bling. Try sticking small sequins, dustings of glitter, or tiny fake jewels onto freshly painted, partially wet nails. The nail polish will act like glue as it dries. You can buy these accessories at a retail store, but you can also make them yourself.

NAIL DECALS

Make your own stick-on nail decorations. Allow extra time for preparation.

What You Need:

- a tablespoon (optional)
- 2 shades of non-glittery nail polish
- wax paper
- a plastic card, such as an old library card
- nail scissors or a hole punch
- tweezers
- Q-tips

Here's How:

1. Pour about 1 tablespoon of your first shade of nail polish onto the wax paper into a small puddle. You want this puddle to be very thick and not very wide.

2. Let the puddle dry for several hours. Make sure the puddle is completely dry before you move on.

3. Use the edge of the plastic card to carefully scrape the dried nail polish blob up from the wax paper. The blob should be flexible, like thin plastic.

4. Carefully cut tiny designs from the dried polish blob with the nail scissors or the hole punch. Set these aside.

5. Paint your nails with one layer of regular nail polish.

6. Let the polish dry a little, but not completely. It should still be tacky and sticky.

7. While polish is still partly wet, use the tweezers to pick up the little cutouts and place them on your nails in the pattern you want.

8. With the Q-tip, smooth out any wrinkles and press down the decals. Let the nails dry completely.

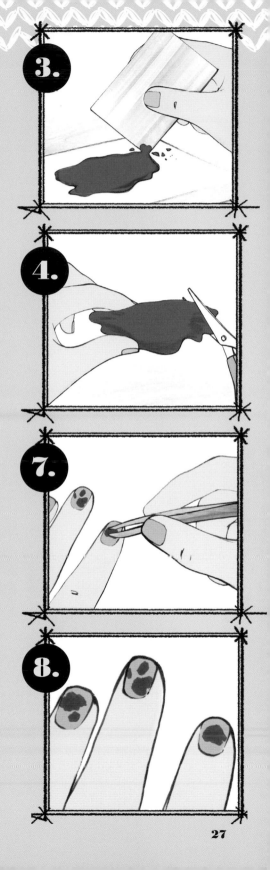

REMOVE AND REBOOT

Be sure to take off your nail polish a few days after applying it. Nails need oxygen, just like the rest of you, and they can't get enough when they're covered with polish. Your nails can turn yellow if you leave polish on for too long.

Most nail polish removers contain a chemical called acetone. Acetone is very effective at removing nail polish fast, but it also releases fumes that can give you a headache. And it can be harmful to your body if you breathe in a lot of it over a period of years.

You can also look for non-acetone nail polish remover. (Check the label.) This type of polish remover is not quite as effective, but it doesn't release harmful fumes. You'll need to rub harder and longer to remove polish with non-acetone polish remover.

No matter which type of remover you use, be sure to take off your nail polish in a room with plenty of fresh air. The chemicals in both types of remover can be unpleasant to breathe.

Getting Rid of Nail Products

Did you know that nail polish is toxic? That's why you should avoid breathing in its fumes. It's also why you shouldn't throw nail products in the trash—or dump them down the sink or the toilet. Even when a nail polish bottle is empty, it still has harmful particles inside it. If these products end up in a landfill or in waterways, they can harm the environment. So how can you get rid of your old polish and remover containers? Take them to a local household hazardous waste collection site. Check online to find the location of your county's collection site.

To remove polish, dip a cotton ball in nail polish remover. Rub the cotton ball over your nails until the polish dissolves. Use a fresh cotton ball when the old one gets covered with polish. Cap your nail polish remover when you're done—never leave it open.

Once all your polish is removed, rinse your fingers and toes in cool water and apply a bit of lotion. Otherwise, the remover can dry out your skin. Now you're ready for the next round of polish! What will you choose this time?

The Real Secret

When you're ready, you can get even more creative with your nail art. Try laying a piece of lace over part of your nail and painting over it, then lifting it off to see what design you've made. Or cover your nail with the edge of a small adhesive bandage, paint over it, and then remove the bandage to reveal tiny polka dots made by the bandage's perforations. How about tracing patterns in partly dried nail polish with a toothpick? You can dip a small sponge, the tip of a bobby pin, or even a pencil eraser in polish and make new shapes.

As you explore new forms of nail art and decoration, don't forget the most important ingredient for great-looking nails: top-notch nail and skin care. Healthy, happy nails will last longer than any coat of polish. And you'll be proud to show them off, whether or not they're all decked out.

GLOSSARY

bacteria: a kind of germ that can, in some forms, be harmful to people

decal: a design that will stick onto another surface

discolored: changed in color due to damage or age

emery board: a strip of cardboard with a rough, sandpaper-like coating

essential oil: a natural oil that smells like the plant it was extracted from

hygiene: things people do to keep their bodies healthy and clean

ingrown: growing into the flesh

manicure: a hand treatment that involves cutting the fingernails, softening the skin, and painting the fingernails

moisturize: to make the skin less dry

nailbrush: a small, stiff brush used to scrub on and around fingernails and toenails

pedicure: a foot treatment that involves trimming the toenails, softening the skin, and painting the toenails

porous: having tiny spaces or holes that air or liquid can pass through

pumice stone: a lightweight piece of rock, that forms when hot lava mixes with water, turns to foam, and hardens

FURTHER INFORMATION

Conrad, Lauren, and Elise Loehnen. *Lauren Conrad Beauty*. New York: HarperCollins, 2012. Get beauty tips from a celebrity.

The Coolest Nail Looks and Designs!—*Seventeen*
http://www.seventeen.com/beauty/celeb-beauty/g1656/crazy-nails/?slide=1
Creative and popular nail art designs are collected in this article.

Geer, Donne, and Ginny Geer. *Nail Candy: 50+ Ideas for Totally Cool Nails*. San Francisco: Weldon Owen, 2013. Find more inspiration for adding bling to your nails.

Haab, Sherri. *Nail Art*. Palo Alto, CA: Klutz, 2009. Decorate your nails with peel-off designs included with this book.

Latchana Kenney, Karen. *Skin Care & Makeup Tips & Tricks*. Minneapolis: Lerner Publications, 2016. Expand your skin care and body beauty routine with this guide to facial fun.

Nail Art: Beginner—Pinterest
https://www.pinterest.com/cutexus/nail-art-beginner/
Check out this gallery of easy-yet-original nail designs to get some new ideas.

Shoket, Ann. *Seventeen Ultimate Guide to Beauty*. Philadelphia: Running Press, 2012. Learn all about nails, skin, and hair from the editors of *Seventeen* magazine.

INDEX

applying nail polish, 16–17

cuticles, 16, 19

foot treatment, 11

getting rid of nail products, 28
glitter nail polish, 17

hangnails, 19

manicures, 4, 18–21

nail art, 24–25, 26–27, 29
nail-biting, 7

nail care tools, 8–9
nail decals, 26–27
nail health, 6–7, 9, 16, 23

organizing and storing supplies, 14–15

pedicures, 4, 18–19, 22–23

removing nail polish, 28–29

skin health, 10–11

types of nail polish, 12–13

PHOTO ACKNOWLEDGMENTS

The images in this book are used with the permission of: © iStockphoto.com/Betty_photo, p. 1 (top); © Nik Merkulov/Shutterstock.com, p. 1 (bottom); © Ruslan Kudrin/Shutterstock.com, p. 2 (all); © HamsterMan/Shutterstock.com, p. 3; © Nik Merkulov/Shutterstock.com, p. 4; © TonyB./Shutterstock.com, p. 5; © Valua Vitaly/Shutterstock.com, p. 6; © morganlstudios/Bigstock.com, p. 7; © gresei/Shutterstock.com, p. 8 (scissors); © Coprid/Shutterstock.com, p. 8 (brush); © iStockphoto.com/cretolamna, p. 8 (nail file); © Everything/Shutterstock.com, p. 8 (foot stone); © Picsfive/Shutterstock.com, p. 10; © starsandspirals/flickr.com (CC BY-SA 2.0), p. 12; © Nik Merkulov/Shutterstock.com, p. 13 (top); © vvoe/Shutterstock.com, p. 13 (middle); © Alexandra Lande/Shutterstock.com, p. 13 (bottom); © iStockphoto.com/shvili, p.14 (all); © Vorobyeva/Shutterstock.com, pp. 16, 32; © Palokha Tetiana/Shutterstock.com, p. 17; © Suljo/Bigstock.com, p. 18; © Sviridov Vitaly/Shutterstock.com, p. 19; © Christos Siatos/Shutterstock.com, p. 20; © Travismanley/Bigstock.com, p. 22 (bottom); © RadvanyiFX/Shutterstock.com, p. 24 (top); © marigo20/Shutterstock.com, p. 24 (bottom); © hightowernrw/Shutterstock.com, p. 26 (top); © iStock/Thinkstock, p. 26 (bottom); © Magnia/Shutterstock.com, p. 28; © iStockphoto.com/WEKWEK, p. 29 (left), 29 (bottom right); © iStockphoto.com/hydrangea100, p. 29 (top right); © Ruslan Kudrin/Shutterstock.com, pp. 30, 31.

Front cover: © Nik Merkulov/Shutterstock.com (nail polish); © iStockphoto.com/Betty_photo (nail polish droplets).

Back cover: © morganlstudios/Bigstock.com (nail clippers); © iStockphoto.com/WEKWEK (nail polish swish); © Nik Merkulov/Shutterstock.com (spilled bottles); © severija/Shutterstock.com (glitter).